Let's Dress Up

and

In the Net

By **Jenny Jinks**

Illustrated by
Lindsay Dale-Scott

The Letter R

Trace the lower and upper case letter with a finger. Sound out the letter.

Down,
up,
around

Down,
up,
around,
down

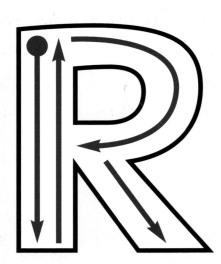

Let's Dress Up

and

In the Net

Maverick
Early Readers

'Let's Dress Up' and 'In the Net'
An original concept by Jenny Jinks
© Jenny Jinks

Illustrated by Lindsay Dale-Scott

Published by MAVERICK ARTS PUBLISHING LTD
Studio 11, City Business Centre, 6 Brighton Road,
Horsham, West Sussex, RH13 5BB
© Maverick Arts Publishing Limited August 2019
+44 (0)1403 256941

A CIP catalogue record for this book is available at the British Library.

ISBN 978-1-84886-612-6

www.maverickbooks.co.uk

Pink

This book is rated as: Pink Band (Guided Reading)
This story is decodable at Letters and Sounds Phase 2.

Some words to familiarise:

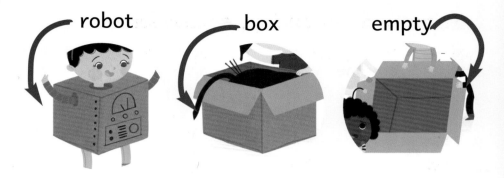

robot   box   empty

High-frequency words:

in   the   a   is

Tips for Reading 'Let's Dress Up'

- Practise the words listed above before reading the story.

- If the reader struggles with any of the other words, ask them to look for sounds they know in the word. Encourage them to sound out the words and help them read the words if necessary.

- After reading the story, ask the reader what Megan dressed up as in the end.

Fun Activity

Make your own robot costumes with cardboard boxes.

Let's Dress Up

Sam looks in the box.

Sam is a bug.

Tim looks in the box.

Tim is a cat.

Kit looks in the box.

Kit is a dragon.

Nick looks in the box.

Nick is a rabbit.

Megan looks in the box.

The box is empty.

Megan is a robot.

The Letter N

Trace the lower and upper case letter with a finger. Sound out the letter.

*Down,
up,
around,
down*

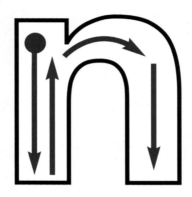

*Down,
up,
down,
up*

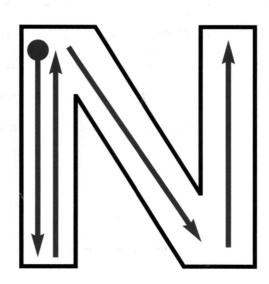

Some words to familiarise:

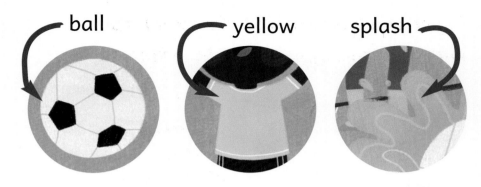

ball   yellow   splash

High-frequency words:

the   is   in   go   it

Tips for Reading 'In the Net'

- Practise the words listed above before reading the story.

- If the reader struggles with any of the other words, ask them to look for sounds they know in the word. Encourage them to sound out the words and help them read the words if necessary.

- After reading the story, ask the reader where the ball is at the end of the story.

Fun Activity

What other sports use a net to catch the ball?

In the Net

Ben kicks the ball.

The ball is in the net.

23

Lil kicks the ball.

The ball is in the net.

Ted kicks the ball.

Splash!

It is not in the net.

The ball is in the net!

Book Bands for Guided Reading

The Institute of Education book banding system is a scale of colours that reflects the various levels of reading difficulty. The bands are assigned by taking into account the content, the language style, the layout and phonics. Word, phrase and sentence level work is also taken into consideration.

Maverick Early Readers are a bright, attractive range of books covering the pink to white bands. All of these books have been book banded for guided reading to the industry standard and edited by a leading educational consultant.

To view the whole Maverick Readers scheme, visit our website at

www.maverickearlyreaders.com

Or scan the QR code above to view our scheme instantly!

Pink
Red
Yellow
Blue
Green
Orange
Turquoise
Purple
Gold
White